Little Book of Big Jerks:

Fast, Fun Illustrated Guide for Dealing with Difficult People

RYN GARGULINSKI

ISBN: 1-937539-03-2
ISBN-13: 978-1-937539-03-0

DEDICATION

This book is dedicated to folks who could use a way to deal with difficult people. I guess that means it's dedicated to everybody.

CONTENTS

Part 1: Cast o' Characters 3

12 DIFFICULT PEOPLE
In alphabetical order

Part 2: Bag o' Tricks 29

12 EASY TOOLS
In no particular order

ACKNOWLEDGMENTS

Oodles of appreciation go to all those who provided encouragement, laughter, input and suggestions as this book slowly meandered forward. People include: Art group leader and members who gave my illustrations a big thumbs up. Writer group members for their fantastic feedback on humor tips, tool inclusion and the almighty shit shield. Mom for helping with the hammer head and other tool ideas. Love-of-my-life Beezel for his on-demand assistance and support.

Introduction

Whether you call them jerks, soul suckers, emotional vampires, pesky persons or pains in the assess, you know one thing for certain: you seem to feel better when difficult people aren't around.

Since avoiding such folks completely is about as likely as being eaten by a shark while driving a bus on dry land, it's essential to find another way to deal. And you've found it with the **Little Book of Big Jerks.**

Here you'll find a two-part tome packed with tips, tricks and humorous tidbits for dealing with difficult people.

- **Part 1** of the book outlines some of the most common jerky types you may run across in your daily life.
- **Part 2** serves up a smorgasbord of tools you can use to retain your sanity after encountering the types in Part1.

Please plunge into this book with that proverbial grain of salt, knowing not all humorous tidbits are meant to be taken literally. Unless, of course, you want to end up in jail.

While it's fine to envision banging a hammer on a pesky person's head in your imagination, for instance, the practice is not so fine when you're doing it for real in your garage. Besides, you might get blood splatter on your car.

Also keep in mind that this book was not created for the sole purpose of bashing difficult people, with a hammer or otherwise. It was created with the intent of helping people change their whole attitude about difficult people in general.

1

How's That?

You know that saying about "If you don't laugh, you cry?"

Instead of automatically crying when a difficult person is nearing your path, you're sure to feel a lot better if you find the humor in the situation. This book was created to help you find the humor – while outlining handy tools that amp up the amusement level even further.

One more big tool that can help with difficult people, and every other aspect of life, is the art of acceptance.

Accept that difficult people exist. Accept that they sometimes might exist right next to you. Accept that you can't change who they are or what they do – but you can change your attitude.

Look for the humor instead of the hatred, and you just might be amazed. Heck, you may even be amazed enough to actually start seeking out difficult people to hang around to test your new attitude.

Just kidding. That hasn't happened yet. Although other wondrous things can happen when you have the right attitude and a bag o' cool tools to deal with difficult people.

--

DISCLAIMER: The difficult people outlined in this book are purely fictional. Any resemblance to real people, living or dead, is merely coincidental – and pretty bad luck for the person.

The tools herein make no claims for anything. They are not meant to replace professional medical assistance, mental therapeutic guidance, or a healthy diet full of leafy, green vegetables and grains.

Part 1:
Cast o' Characters

ARGUMENTATIVE ANNA	BACKSTABBING BEATRICE	BLATHERING BETTY
BORING BORIS	CANTANKEROUS CONNIE	COMPLAINING CHARLES
DRAMATIC DOLLY	GIMME GINA	NEGATIVE NELLIE
ONE-UP OPHELIA	TAG-ALONG TOM	WOEFUL WILLIAM

Argumentative Anna

Tell her the sky is blue, and she'll argue that it's really a greenish-yellowish azure.

Argumentative Anna

Argumentative Anna is an expert on everything, or so she thinks. And the first thing she knows is that whatever you know is wrong. It doesn't matter that she never rode a horse, painted an awning or flown a plane, she'll tell the cowboy his saddle is too tight, tell the awning painter the color is not right and tell the pilot he's doing the landing thing all wrong.

3 Giveaway Traits:

- Constantly barges in with her input, even if she has no idea about the topic at hand
- Tells you you're wrong, even if you happen to agree with her
- Argues about things that have basis in scientific fact, like that silly idea about the earth being round

How to Deal:

Tell her she's right. Absolutely right.

Backstabbing Beatrice

Tell her the sky is blue, and she'll say you're so amazing to notice. Then she'll go tell everyone else you suck.

Backstabbing Beatrice

Backstabbing Beatrice is a major staple at every high school, but you can also find her well into adulthood. She pops up as committee members, coworkers and neighbors who are sweet as pie to your face but talk sour grapes behind your back.

If ever confronted about bad-mouthing you, Beatrice will, of course, say the person who told you that is a big, fat liar who sucks.

3 Giveaway Traits:
- Flatters you to sickening lengths in an attempt to throw you off-guard and earn your trust
- Constantly tries to gather intimate information she can later blab to the entire office, block or neighborhood association
- Has quotes like "Rumor has it" and "Et, tu, Brute?" in her email signature line

How to Deal:

Never turn your back.

Blathering Betty

Tell her the sky is blue, and she won't hear you. She's too busy blabbing on and on about her cat, her boss, the cyst on her left butt cheek or something else you care absolutely nothing about.

Blathering Betty

Encountering Blathering Betty is akin to being smothered by a landslide of lava, except instead of being suffocated by hot, bubbly liquid you're suffocated by words.

There are no such things as discussions or conversations in her presence, just ongoing monologues about her mom's housedress, her cat's toenails or something else that has at least a dozen tangents she needs to explain in excruciating detail.

3 Giveaway Traits:
- Lures you into a false sense of discussion by briefly asking how you are before she launches into her jabbering
- Neither comments on or even listens to the answer to how you are
- If you answer the phone and it's her, you may as well cancel your plans for the next two weeks

How to Deal:

Learn to nod in just the right places without actually listening to a thing.

Boring Boris

Tell him the sky is blue, and he'll say blue is the same color as his childhood tricycle – then launch into a tedious explanation of tricycle wheel spokes.

Boring Boris

If you're suffering from insomnia, Boring Boris is the ideal pal. That's because everything he says pretty much puts you to sleep.

Boris has the bizarre ability to make even the most exciting stories of murder, mayhem and debauchery sound boring. And he'll repeat the exact same stories again and again – and again.

3 Giveaway Traits:
- Drones on and on about things like the history of nickels and components used in AstroTurf
- Has a lifetime membership to the museum of metal shelving units
- Once brought a paperclip to show-and-tell

How to Deal:

Drink coffee. Lots of coffee. Better yet, don't. Consider Boris a chance to take a much-needed nap.

Cantankerous Connie

Tell her the sky is blue, and she'll say she can't see it because your tree branches are blocking her view over her fence – and when will your durn dogs stop barking?!

Cantankerous Connie

Cantankerous Connie is the nosy, bellyaching neighbor who always has something ornery to say. And it's usually something connected to your home or yard.

Your dogs are too loud. Your barbecue is too smoky. Your tree branches are too far over her fence. Your car is parked too close to her curb. And by the way, can she borrow your ladder?

3 Giveaway Traits:
- The mere sound of her voice makes you – and your dogs – run inside and hide
- Always lurking around pretending to be busy when she's really just a busybody
- Takes pictures of things she thinks are wrong with your home, yard and vehicles then sends them to the HOA

How to Deal:

Build a bigger fence.

Complaining Charles

Tell him the sky is blue, and he'll complain it's not the same shade it had been six weeks ago on Tuesday.

Complaining Charles

No matter how glorious, wonderful or absolutely awesome a situation is, Complaining Charles will find reason to complain. The blue sky is not blue enough. The dazzling sunset started too late. And the melt-your-heart, cute-as-a-button puppy? Well, that thing pees on the floor.

Complaining Charles not only goes through life with the proverbial glass half-empty, but he'll complain there are fingerprint smudges on the rim.

3 Giveaway Traits:
- Can find something wrong with everything
- Never has a solution or desire to change things
- Frequently ends up in boss or managerial positions

How to Deal:

Tell him there's a bright spot: he's eventually going to die.

Dramatic Dolly

Tell her the sky is blue, and she'll immediately screech that it's falling and can't you see the pressure she's under?!

Dramatic Dolly

If the world were indeed a stage, Dramatic Dolly would nab the starring role. She's the type that thrives on creating drama around the most mundane situations and activities, like an off-center throw rug or buying socks.

An outing with Dramatic Dolly typically involves lots of screeching, hyperventilating and a panicked whirlwind of activity as she swirls around in a tizzy about whatever she thinks is irrevocably wrong at the moment.

3 Giveaway Traits:
- Calls in sick to work if she gets a hangnail
- Feels her entire life is ruined if she breaks a shoelace
- Wouldn't know a real tragedy if it hit her in the ass

How to Deal:

Hand her an Oscar (or at least a Tony).

Gimme Gina

Tell her the sky is blue, and she'll ask to borrow your blue sweater.

Gimme Gina

Whether it's a ride home, a piece of chewing gum or your last dollar, Gimme Gina is always after something. And she's pretty good at getting it. She has a wide range of manipulation tactics designed to evoke sympathy, sisterhood or the strong urge just to give her something just so she'll go away.

But do beware. Give this gal the proverbial inch and she'll take about 10,000 miles – and your last dollar.

3 Giveaway Traits:

- Usually gloms on to the new kid in town who is not yet savvy to her habits
- Good at creating sob stories that often involve sickly relatives or dying pets
- Never reciprocates, never even offers to

How to Deal:

Tell her the only thing you feel like giving her is the plague.

Negative Nellie

Tell her the sky is blue, and she'll say even the bluest sky can't hide all the cancer-causing chemicals swirling around our atmosphere.

Negative Nellie

Negative Nellie has a keen sense for sniffing out anything remotely positive – and then squashing it like a bug. She's the ultimate queen of the negative attitude. And that attitude reigns supreme by putting a negative spin on existing situations as well as making negative projections for any situation to come.

Your next great idea is destined to flop. Your trip to the tropics is going to land you with malaria – that is, of course, if you even make it there. You're plane just might crash on the way, you know.

3 Giveaway Traits:
- Throws a sopping wet blanket over every sparkle of excitement
- Lives by the rule that if something can go wrong, it will – and she'd be glad to tell you all about it
- Makes small children cry

How to Deal:

Put ex-lax in her orange juice.

One-Up Ophelia

Tell her the sky is blue, and she'll say she already noticed it this morning, way ahead of you – and did she mention she almost went to Harvard?

One-Up Ophelia

You could be having the most spectacular moment of your life, but it'll never match up to the what just happened to One-Up Ophelia. This gal spends her days trumping anything and everything anyone does, making others feel little so she can feel big.

Your son got an A? Hers got an A+. Got new carpet in your den? She got new carpet, furniture, and a life-size statue of Carol Channing. Just received word you're in the running for a Pulitzer Prize? Heck, she's already won two of those ole things – and she's avidly working on her third.

3 Giveaway Traits:
- Is incapable of being happy for anyone else's good fortune, or even pretending to be
- Driven to make people feel unworthy and small
- Has a favorite one-upper she'll mention every single time, like the fact that she almost went to Harvard

How to Deal:

Pretend you have no clue what Harvard is.

Tag-Along Tom

Tell him the sky is blue, and he'll beg to come with you to go check it out.

Tag-Along Tom

Remember how your little brother or sister would try to follow you around wherever you went? Tag-Along Tom is like that, except you can't even call on Mom to save you. One of the biggest dangers is mentioning any type of plans when Tag-Along Tom is within a radius of up to about 20 miles.

Not only will he sidle over asking for all the details, but he'll attempt to wheedle his way into the event. It doesn't matter if the outing is a pool party and he can't swim, a camping trip and he hates mosquitoes, or a friendly visit to your neighborhood gastroenterologist. Tag-Along Tom wants to come along.

3 Giveaway Traits:
- Has a way of opening his eyes really big, like a lost puppy, so you'll feel bad and invite him along
- Doesn't realize the lost puppy look worked a heck of a lot better back when he was 5, not now at 45
- Starts most conversations with either, "What time are we meeting?" or "When's the next party?"

How to Deal:

Tell him to meet you in Mexico for the weekend. Then quickly head to Canada.

Woeful William

Tell him the sky is blue, and he'll lament how it never stays blue for long and his roof leaks when it rains.

Woeful William

Just like everything King Midas touched turn to gold, everything Woeful William touches turns to, well, crap. This guy is a magnet for really bad luck.

His roof leaks. His car stalls. His pants rip. His cat hates him. At one time you actually had sympathy for the chap until you read somewhere that people with woeful outlooks actually cause their own bad luck. Now you just feel like shaking him.

3 Giveaway Traits:
- Inspired a record number of sad country songs
- Has had a long lineup of pets that hated him, died tragically, or both
- Always has an empty chair on either side of him at group lunches and dinners

How to Deal:

Stick a "Kick Me" sign on his back.

Part 2:
Bag o' Tricks

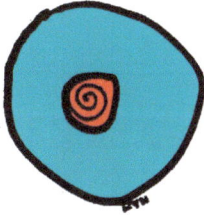

SHIT SHIELD	**SEAPARTION SATELLITE**	**BRILLIANT BALLOON**
HUBBA BUBBLE	**SUPER SWATTER**	**BARF BAG**
SPIRIT SCRAPER	**MENTAL FLOSS**	**PREDICTION METER**
HAMMER HEAD	**SHOWER SCREAM**	**HOT BATH**

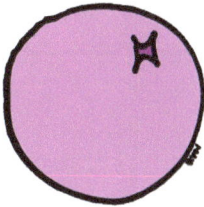

29

Shit Shield

Shit Shield

No, it's not a shield made out of shit. It's a shield made to protect you from shit. Big, heavy and made out of an impenetrable material like Kevlar, the shit shield can be held up between you and anyone giving you shit.

How it Works:

Once the shield is firmly in place, all the shit spewing from the person on the other side simply hits and slides on down the shield. No muss. No fuss. And no stinky stuff stuck to your clothing. Hose it down often.

Separation Satellite

Separation Satellite

More commonly known as a separation object, this tool is used by psychics to ensure they retain strong boundaries and are not polluted with evil or unwanted energy while they're doing a reading or otherwise tapping into the psychic realm.

The satellite roams around your orbit, automatically deflecting negative energy and shooting it back at its source like a high-speed hockey puck. The object can be anything you like: a flower, a lollipop, a baby giraffe. You can even make it be something big and menacing, like a dragon, although he's going to be much more costly to feed.

How it Works:

Simply call upon your separation satellite when you feel anyone is trying to cross your boundaries or infuse you with unwanted energy. Your satellite is designed to pop into place, autonomously moving around to deflect and protect where it's needed most.

Brilliant Balloon

Brilliant Balloon

This tool works particularly well at dysfunctional family gatherings, boring business meetings, or other bothersome places where you end up stuck for hours with no escape. Even if you can't physically escape, the brilliant balloon gives you a mental escape.

Instead of staying down on the ground amidst all the craziness, hop on the brilliant balloon to go floating up into the sky where you get a birds-eye view of all the hullabaloo beneath you.

How it Works:

The moment you feel the walls closing in, envision a brilliant balloon coming to save you. It's huge. It's handsome. And it has a cozy basket lined with maroon velveteen where you get to sit.

Take a seat and let the balloon go up, up, up in the air where you're totally safe, totally detached and neither affected nor afflicted by all the goings-on below. Add to the amusement by pretending you're watching a really bad TV sitcom – just make sure you don't accidentally guffaw out loud in the middle of the boring business meeting.

Hubba Bubble

Hubba Bubble

Similar to the brilliant balloon, the hubba bubble detaches you from the difficult people and situations surrounding you. But unlike the brilliant balloon, you get to stay on the ground. Ideal alternative if you happen to be driving or afraid of heights.

The hubba bubble is a giant bubble that keeps out the bad, kind of like an oxygen tent but in a wider array of colors.

How it Works:

Let the bubble appear and surround you anytime you're feeling like the world is too much with us. You'll soon feel comforted and at ease, protected in an impenetrable membrane that only lets love and your dogs get through.

Make your hubba bubble any color you like. Give it extra power by singing the hubba bubble song:

I am in a bubble; I am in a bubble.
I am in a bubble; a bubble covers me.

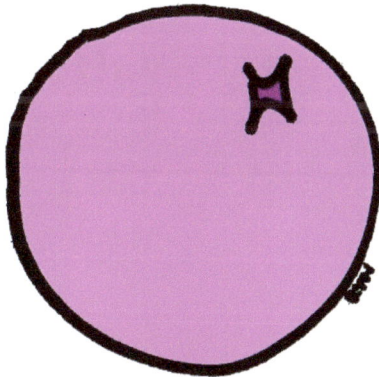

Super Swatter

Super Swatter

While many tools let you passively protect yourself, the super swatter allows you to actively defend yourself. A good tool for those totally fed up or prone to violence.

All you need to do is imagine a giant fly swatter about the size of Memphis, complete with an easy-grip handle, lightweight build and pliable yet strong swatting surface.

How it Works:

Picture the difficult person as a fat, buzzing fly. Then grab your super swatter and go for it!

Barf Bag

Barf Bag

Originally invented by airlines to preserve seat cushions, the barf bag works equally as well as a handy tool to preserve your sanity. Difficult people can often take you by surprise, spewing their garbage in your direction before you even know what's happening.

By the time they're done with you, you're definitely ready to purge. And the barf bag is the perfect tool in which to do it.

How it Works:

The moment you're able to take a breather, find a quiet, peaceful location. Take out your barf bag, opening it carefully. The vomit out every last morsel of garbage the difficult person just fed you.

Discard and replace as needed.

Spirit Scraper

Spirit Scraper

You know how gum or dog poo sticks to your shoe? Well, the same thing can happen with difficult people. All their gooey, slimy energy can end up stuck to your spirit, leaving a grimy film that just won't budge.

Budge it off with the spirit scraper, a tool that kind of looks like a window squeegee but with a much harder edge. The edge is made of diamond, in fact, and it has the power to whisk away any lingering crud that may have been deposited on your soul.

How it Works:

Due to its convenient size, you can pull out the spirit scraper any time you feel the difficult people sludge start to build up on any part of your spirit. Start scraping away at affected areas until your spirit is as crisp, clean and clear as the day you were born.

Rinse scraper frequently in hot water. Use chlorine bleach as needed.

Mental Floss

Mental Floss

Similar to dental floss but for the brain, mental floss cleans out built-up crud that's been deposited by difficult people over time. Leave the crud to fester, and your mind's deep pockets and crevices are subject to decay – or worse.

You could find yourself behaving as negatively as Nellie, as woefully as William, or begging for favors as vehemently as Gina.

How it Works:

Imagine a long, thin piece of floss that you insert in one ear and out the other. Grasp one end of the strand in each hand, pulling it back and forth several times while it's stretched taut through your skull. Make a swishing sound for added effectiveness.

Your mental floss can be waxed or unwaxed, any flavor you like. Dispose of floss promptly after use so your pets don't accidentally get ahold of it and choke.

Prediction Meter

Prediction Meter

The prediction meter is a coping tool that doubles as a game you can play by yourself or with friends. The overall aim of the game is to predict something the difficult person will say or do based on past behaviors and habits. Get it right, and you win!

How it Works:

Pull out the prediction meter whenever you're about to encounter a difficult person, and make any prediction you wish. Examples include predicting:

- How many times One-Up Ophelia will mention Harvard in the first 12 minutes of conversation
- What Negative Nellie will say to bash your latest idea
- What excuse Gimme Gina will use for needing to borrow money today

You get the idea. Hours of enjoyment. In fact, the prediction meter can bring such a thrill to your encounter with difficult people that you may altogether forget you're supposed to be bothered or annoyed by them.

Hammer Head

Hammer Head

My mom came up with this one, and it's both supremely simple and supremely effective.

How it Works:

Envision a hammer. Then imagine you're bashing the difficult person in the head with it. Repeat as needed.

Done.

Shower Scream

Shower Scream

Another incredibly simple and effective tool is the shower scream. This tool is a must if you've been around difficult people for extended periods without a chance to revive.

How it Works:

Get into a hot shower. Do your usual hair wash, body lather, and other physical cleansing as usual. Then stick your head directly beneath the shower head and let out a prolonged, piercing, penetrating scream.

Scream from the belly. Scream from the gut. Scream from the bottom of your soul. Scream as long, loud and strenuously as you need. Then get out, dry off, and go on with your day.

If a shower's not possible or convenient yet you really need a scream, alternatives include screaming into a pillow, screaming in an alleyway or, as my friend Wendy does, screaming in your car.

Hot Bath

Hot Bath

The hot bath is the opposite of the shower scream. Instead of heading into the bathroom to scream out your agony, you head into the bathroom to soak away your woes.

How it Works:

Hook up your favorite soaking solution, whether it's bath salts, an oatmeal soak or Mr. Bubble. My fave is Epsom salt mixed with sea salt mixed with a hefty dose of lavender essential oil.

Lie back in the tub on your over-priced floating bath pillow and close your eyes. Envision the water molecules entering into every crevice of every cell in your body, swirling around in little clockwise circles, and then exiting after they've left you thoroughly clean and free of flotsam, jetsam and any other detritus and debris you may have picked up from all those difficult people.

Hooray and Congratulations!

If you started this book at the beginning and read it all the way through, you're prepped, armed and more than ready to take on any difficult people who may come ambling your way.

If you started at the end of the book, like my sister-in-law does, then you're reading this page prematurely. But we love you anyway.

Once you do get through the entire book, you'll be equipped to:

- Instantly identify difficult people before they get their claws into you
- Know when to decline invitations that could turn into painful situations
- Protect yourself from woeful wailings, bothersome blathering and other negative vibes
- Transform tragedy into comedy – while having fun along the way

ABOUT THE AUTHOR

Ryn Gargulinski is a writer, artist and animal lover who has insider knowledge on difficult people – since she definitely used to be one. While not by any means perfect at present, she does make a conscious effort to focus on positive over negative, compassion over complaints, and wonder over woe.

Backed by a BFA in Creative Writing, MA in English literature and numerous years on the journalism scene, Ryn works freelance through her writing and art business of Ryndustries. Check out more info at ryngargulinski.com. Go shopping at the Rynski Etsy shop at rynski.etsy.com.

www.ingramcontent.com/pod-product-compliance
Lightning Source LLC
Chambersburg PA
CBHW041214270326
41930CB00001B/21